THE BAT BOOK

DISCOVER THE SECRET WORLD OF BATS

Every evening at nightfall, bats take to the sky, swooping and swerving in the dark. Like tiny superheroes, these busy animals often go completely unnoticed. But even when we don't know that they are around, bats play an important role in keeping the natural world healthy.

Let's find out about bats and why they are important...

WHERE DO BATS LIVE?

Bats are found all over the world except for the North and South Poles, where it is too cold for them to live.

THERE ARE OVER 1,300 SPECIES OF BAT.

With so many different types, bats have adapted to live in nearly all environments. Whether you are in a city, a forest, or the desert, bats can be found nearby.

Bats are nearly everywhere and have an effect on us all.

Hoary bats live in forests.

Free-tailed bats live in cities.

Desert long-eared bats live in deserts.

SOME BATS ARE BIG...

The biggest bat, the **GIANT GOLDEN-CROWNED FLYING FOX**, has a wingspan of more than 5ft (150cm).

SOME BATS ARE SMALL...

The cute **BUMBLEBEE BAT** gets its name from its tiny size. Its body is about the size of a large bumblebee and it weighs no more than 1/10oz (2g).

SOME BATS ARE FAST...

The **MEXICAN FREE-TAILED BAT** is the fastest of all bats and can fly at a speed of 100 miles (160km) per hour.

SOME BATS CAN SING...

Like a songbird, the **GREATER SAC-WINGED BAT** sings to defend its territory. Its loud song can be heard more than 328ft (100m) away.

SOME BATS LIVE LONG LIVES...

BRANDT'S BAT can live for 40 years or longer. That's nearly 10 times longer than most other animals of the same size.

SOME BATS HAVE STYLE...

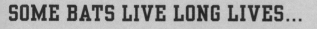

The hairs on the male **CHAPIN'S FREE-TAILED BAT'S** head stick up like a spiked hairdo.

WHAT IS A BAT?

A bat is the only **MAMMAL** that can fly.
Mammals are a large group of animals that include humans.

Like humans, bats are warm-blooded, have a bony skeleton, and give birth to live babies instead of laying eggs.

DURING THE DAY BATS ARE ASLEEP

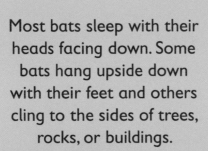

Most bats sleep with their heads facing down. Some bats hang upside down with their feet and others cling to the sides of trees, rocks, or buildings.

DURING THE NIGHT BATS ARE AWAKE

Most bats are **NOCTURNAL**, which means they are active when it is dark. This is when they look for food, such as insects.

Most bats live together in a large group, called a **COLONY**.

The place where bats live is called a **ROOST**. In the roost bats sleep, groom themselves, and have babies.

WHAT DO BATS DO...

WHEN IT IS COLD?

Some bats live in parts of the world where there are cold winters. During these chilly months, there is not enough food around for bats to eat. To survive the winter, they hibernate, which means they go into a deep sleep, living off the fat they have stored up over the warmer months.

WHEN IT IS WARM?

During warm nights, bats are busy finding and eating food such as insects. Female bats also gather together once a year to have babies. Each female bat gives birth to one baby, called a pup. She cares for her pup by feeding it with milk until the young bat is ready to fly.

WHAT DO BATS LOOK LIKE?

There is an amazing variety of bat species and they all look very different. But there are two main groups of bats: megabats and microbats.

MEGABATS LIVE in tropical and subtropical areas in Africa, Asia, and Australia, where it is warm and humid.

MEGABATS EAT mostly fruit, but some eat pollen and a sugary syrup from flowers called nectar.

MEGABATS

Most megabats grow to be much **LARGER** than
...... microbats.

They **WRAP** their wings around their bodies when roosting.......

Spectacled flying fox

Megabats have **BIG EYES.**

Megabats have **LONG SNOUTS.**

8

MICROBATS

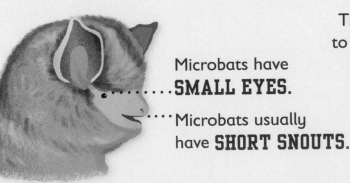

Daubenton's bat

..... Some have **TAILS**.

..... Most microbats are **SMALLER** than megabats.

They mostly like to fold their wings **ALONGSIDE** their bodies.

Microbats have **SMALL EYES**.

Microbats usually have **SHORT SNOUTS**.

MICROBATS LIVE nearly everywhere in the world.

MICROBATS EAT mostly insects, but there are some types that eat fruit, nectar, other small animals, or blood.

FUNNY FACES

Microbats can have curiously shaped ears and noses, which help them to hear and make sounds.

Yellow-winged bat

Horseshoe bat

Sword-nosed bat

A BAT'S BODY

Bats have special features that make them experts at flying and finding prey.

thumb

A bat's **THUMB** is short and has a claw on the end, which it uses to climb up trees.

second finger

forearm

Like us, a bat has four fingers and a thumb. But a bat's fingers are long, and skin stretches between them to make a **WING**.

third finger

The **FINGER BONES** inside a bat's wing are light and bendy. Having flexible finger bones and joints means that bats are more agile when flying than most birds are.

fourth finger

fifth finger

Curved, sharp **CLAWS** on a bat's toes help it to hook onto surfaces while hanging upside down.

Some bats can see very well with their **EYES**. Others rely more on their hearing and sense of smell to know what's around them.

Small, sharp **TEETH** help a bat to bite into fruits or prey.

A bat has **FUR** that keeps it warm.

Short-nosed fruit bat

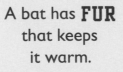

HOW DO BATS FLY?

The bones in a bat's wing are more similar to the bones in a human arm and hand than to the bones in a bird's wing. When bats fly, they can move their wings almost like we can move our hands. This makes their wings very flexible and makes bats very acrobatic flyers.

bat wing

human arm and hand

bird wing

WHY DO BATS HANG UPSIDE DOWN?

Bats can't launch off the ground into flight like birds do, so instead they climb to a high point, hang upside down, and fall into flight. Hanging upside down is the perfect position for bats to quickly fly away whenever they need to.

BUT ISN'T HANGING UPSIDE DOWN TIRING?

If we were to hang from our hands for hours, our muscles would get very tired. But bats can hang upside down without any effort at all. This is because their leg muscles can relax while their feet are clenched. A bat only uses its muscles to pull its claws open.

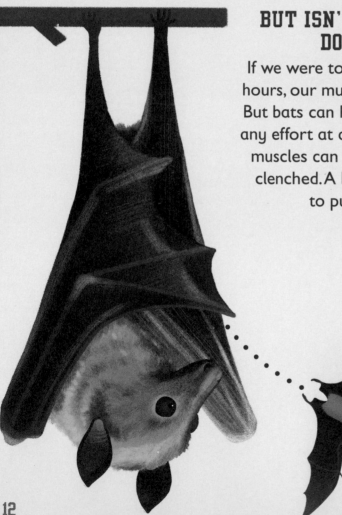

Indian flying fox

WHERE DO BATS HANG OUT?

The ability to hang or cling upside down means that bats can choose to rest in safe places where other animals won't find them. The most common places where bats roost are in trees, buildings, and caves.

Small microbats roost in narrow holes found in **TREE TRUNKS** and branches.

Megabats roost at the tops of tall **TREES**, too high up for predators such as snakes to find them.

In Australia, around 30,000 **grey-headed flying foxes** can be found roosting together in one tree canopy.

BUILDINGS such as houses, churches, and barns make good homes for bats. They will roost in small gaps in roofs, walls, and bricks. A little bat can enter a hole as tiny as ½in (1cm) wide.

Bats like caves, mines, and other **UNDERGROUND** hiding places that are dark and quiet. They hang from ridges in cave ceilings.

Bracken Cave in Texas, is home to the world's largest colony of bats, with around 20 million **Mexican free-tailed bats** roosting there.

13

UNUSUAL HANGOUTS

While most bats find shelter and safe places to rest in trees, buildings, and caves, other bats have found some more unusual places to call home.

The **sucker-footed bat** has suction pads on its wrists and ankles and can roost on the smooth and shiny leaves of the traveller's tree.

Tent-making bats nibble and fold leaves to build their own tent for roosting.

The **lesser bamboo bat** is one of the world's smallest mammals and roosts in the hollow stems of bamboo.

The **painted bat**
roosts in the nests
of sunbirds.

Hardwicke's woolly bat
roosts inside carnivorous
pitcher plants. The plant
gives the bat shelter while
the bat's poop helps the
plant to grow.

WHAT DO BATS EAT?

With over 1,300 species of bat, there is a huge variety of food that bats eat. Many bats eat fruit, nectar, or insects, but there are others with a more unusual taste in food.

Many bats eat **FRUIT** and **NECTAR** from plants.

Cashew apple

Nectar is a sticky, sweet liquid that is found inside flowers.

Dates

The tube-lipped nectar bat's tongue is longer than its own body. It uses its tongue to reach into flowers and lap up **nectar.**

Most microbats survive off a diet of **INSECTS**, by eating lots of moths, beetles, and other bugs every night.

Gypsy moth

June bug

Katydid

Leaf-cutter

Stinkbug

Some microbats eat **SMALL ANIMALS** such as centipedes, fish, frogs, and even scorpions.

Out of all the bats, only three species are vampire bats that eat the **blood** of mammals and birds. Vampire bats make a painless cut from which they lick blood.

While the sting of an **Arizona bark scorpion** could kill a human, the pallid bat is immune to the sting and eats the venomous creatures for dinner.

Frog-eating bats learn the different calls of **frogs** to know whether the frog is poisonous or if it will make a tasty meal.

Fish and shrimp are food for Mexican fishing bats. These bats are known as marine mammals because they fly out to sea every night to catch food.

Heart-nosed bats can hear the footsteps of a **dung beetle** on sand from 6ft (2m) away.

Giant desert centipede

HOW DO BATS FIND FOOD IN THE DARK?

You might have heard the phrase "blind as a bat," but not only can bats see with their eyes, many of them can also use sound to "see" in the dark. Using sound to find things is called ECHOLOCATION. Like whales and dolphins, bats use echolocation to find food.

We can't hear the noise that bats make because the sounds are too high-pitched for our ears to hear.

HOW DO BATS USE SOUND TO SEE?

Bats that use echolocation make chirping sounds as they fly.

↓

The chirping sounds travel in waves across the air, and these sound waves bounce off objects.

↓

When the sound bounces back, the chirp sound is repeated. This is called an echo.

↓

Bats listen to the echoes to know where things are in the dark.

Eastern red bat

The pink lines are the bat's chirp sound.

The dotted lines are the returning echo.

When the bat's chirp sound bounces off an insect and the bat hears the echo, it will know…

WHERE the insect is.

What **SHAPE** the insect is.

Which **DIRECTION** the insect is flying in.

MOTHS VS BATS

Bats use echolocation to catch moths in the dark. But some moths have interesting ways to confuse bats and avoid getting eaten.

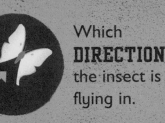

Big brown bat

Bats don't eat the wings of a moth, so they aim for the body when they strike. The long moth tails confuse bats, so that they strike for the tails instead of the body, and the moth can fly away unharmed.

The moon moth has long tails on its rear wings for a good reason. Moths with longer tails are more likely to escape from a bat.

19

WHY ARE **BATS IMPORTANT?**

Bats don't get enough credit for all their hard work. Every night, while they are busy finding food, bats are also doing some very important jobs that benefit our lives, too. Bats pollinate plants, disperse seeds, and eat insects that could damage our crops.

Let's find out more about how bats help us and the environment...

WHAT IS POLLINATION?

The process of moving pollen from one flower to another is called pollination. But flowers can't move pollen by themselves, so they need the help of wind, insects, or other animals, such as bats. When a flower is pollinated, its seeds can start to grow. More than 500 types of plant are pollinated by bats.

HOW DO BATS POLLINATE FLOWERS?

Lesser long-nosed bat

1.
Using echolocation, sight, or smell, the bat finds a flower.

2.
The bat buries its head in the flower to eat the nectar. Pollen falls off the flower's **stamen**.

Stamen

The stamen is the part of the flower that makes pollen.

Organ pipe cactus

3.
After visiting the flower, the bat's fluffy head is covered in pollen.

4.
The bat visits another flower to eat nectar.

Stigma

The stigma is the part of the flower that collects pollen.

5.
At the next flower, the pollen falls off the bat's fur and gets stuck on the sticky part of the flower, called the **stigma.**

6.
The pollen enters the flower at the stigma and grows a tube to the ovary.

..... **pollen**

.... **tube**

Here, it meets the egg.

.... **ovary**

..... **egg**

After the pollen has joined with the egg, the egg starts to become a **seed.**

When planted, the seed can grow into a new **plant.**

.... **seed**

BATS AS SEED DISPERSERS

Plants don't just need bats for pollination. They also need bats and other animals to spread their seeds. The seeds that bats scatter far and wide will grow into new plants. Bats spread the seeds of many plants in the rain forest, including avocado, cashew, and fig trees.

While fruit bats love to feast on the juicy flesh of fruits, they don't always like to eat the seeds. As they chomp away, the seeds drop to the ground.

In tropical forests, fruits like these wild figs grow on trees. All wild fruits contain seeds.

Seeds

Sometimes bats will swallow the seeds while eating fruits. The hard seeds pass through the bats' bodies and come out in their poop. Their droppings are scattered across the forest.

Epauletted fruit bat

Sometimes bats carry fruits from tree to tree, dropping the seeds all around the forest as they eat.

Bats' droppings contain fruit seeds, as well as all the nutrients that seeds need to grow into healthy new trees.

BATS HELP LOTS OF IMPORTANT PLANTS TO GROW

In tropical climates there are bats that love to drink nectar from flowers, as well as bats that love to eat fruit. These bats have an important ecological role because they pollinate plants and spread their seeds, so new plants can grow. Many of these plants produce fruits that we eat, including some of our favorites: mangoes, figs, and bananas.

Flying fox

Some megabats love to eat **GUAVA** and they spread the plant's seeds.

The famously smelly **DURIAN** fruit needs bats for pollination.

Flying foxes carry **MANGOES** back to their roost, eat the pulp, and drop the large seeds to the ground.

The seeds of **PASSION FRUITS** are spread by bats.

The tropical fruit **PAPAYA** has its seeds spread by fruit bats.

In Southeast Asia, wild **BANANA** flowers are pollinated by cave nectar bats, which hang onto the large, red bud while drinking nectar from rows of small, yellow flowers. When pollinated, these flowers will grow into bananas.

FIGS are a delicious food for fruit bats, and bats are important because they spread the fig tree's seeds. Fig trees are also used to make paper, timber, and medicine.

Cave nectar bat

BATS ON THE FARM

Plants that we grow on farms for products like food and clothes are called crops. Farmers like to keep hungry insects away from the crops. Luckily, they get help from bats. Some bats love to eat insects and can eat over a thousand bugs each night.

In the United States and Mexico, there's a hungry type of moth, called a **corn earworm moth.** It likes to eat crops, including cotton, artichokes, and corn.

Corn earworm moths are **Mexican free-tailed bats'** favorite meal. A single bat can consume its own body weight in insects during one night.

These foods are all grown with the help of bats that keep insects away:

Chocolate made from cocoa beans

Sugar made from sugarcane

Almonds

Farmers rely on free-tailed bats to stop the moths from damaging their crops. The bats' help also allows the farmers to use less pesticides to keep insects away.

Pesticides are harmful because they kill large numbers of insects that other animals need to eat to survive. Bats are important because they reduce the amount of pesticides that are used.

Walnuts

Rice

Pears

Cucumbers

BATS KEEP DIFFERENT ECOSYSTEMS HEALTHY

An ecosystem is a natural environment where plants and animals live together and interact with each other for survival. Bats are essential to ecosystems because they pollinate plants and disperse seeds, which provides food and shelter for other animals too.

Let's find out how bats are vital to ecosystems all over the world...

BATS IN THE RAIN FOREST

Rain forests clean the air that we breathe and are home to about half of the world's plant and animal species. But all around the world, people are cutting down trees in the rain forest. This leaves bare areas of ground where forest animals are unable to survive. But bats help these cleared areas to grow back.

HOW DO BATS HELP REFORESTATION?

1.
In South America, bats drop seeds in a cleared area of the rain forest. From these seeds, plants will grow.

2.
The plants create shelter for more plants to grow around them.

3.
These plants attract birds and primates, who also eat fruits and drop seeds in the area.

4.
Eventually, this leads to the bare area of forest being restored, which provides a home for lots of animals again.

BATS IN THE DESERT

As well as rain forests, bats are essential to desert ecosystems, where it is hot and dry. Without bats to pollinate desert cacti, many animals would not be able to find food or shelter.

During the night, the Mexican saguaro cactus' flowers are pollinated by bats. The cactus then grows plump, red fruits that are an important food for many animals.

ANIMALS THAT EAT THE CACTUS' FRUIT:

Jackrabbit

Desert tortoise

Peccary

These animals eat the cactus' seeds and spread them in places where new cacti can grow.

ANIMALS THAT FIND SHELTER FROM THE CACTUS:

 Gila woodpeckers make holes in the cactus' trunk to nest in.

 Elf owls also roost inside the woodpeckers' holes.

 Sap beetles live inside the cactus' flowers.

BATS IN THE SAVANNA

In the hot, dry African savanna stands a tall baobab tree. This tree is more than 2,000 years old and is known as "the tree of life" because it gives shelter and food to many animals. The tree stands with dozens like itself, and bats help the baobab trees by pollinating their flowers.

Once a year and for one night only, the baobab trees bloom. In the dark, their large white flowers open and release their fruity scent to attract bats. Bats pollinate the flowers.

African baobab tree

Wahlberg's epauletted fruit bat

Once bats pollinate the trees, fruits filled with seeds grow from their branches. These fruits are eaten by many animals, such as birds and monkeys.

Birds and monkeys spread the trees' seeds far and wide across the savanna and new baobab trees grow.

The trees provide shade and shelter. Weaver birds build nests among the branches, while bats and owls roost in the hollows.

Baobab trees are vital for the survival of animals when water is hard to come by. Elephants chew on the bark because the trees store water in their thick trunks.

Humans also make use of nearly every part of the trees:

The leaves are eaten like spinach.

The fruit is made into juice and jam.

The seeds are pressed for cooking oil.

The roots are made into a red dye.

Bark is used to make rope and baskets.

WHY ARE BATS IN DECLINE?

Bats live quiet lives and go mostly unnoticed, but behind the scenes they are playing a vital role in keeping the natural world healthy. But sadly, many important bat species are vulnerable or endangered.

Let's find out what challenges bats are facing...

MYTHS AND MISUNDERSTANDINGS

Sadly, a lot of people hear of vampire bats and think that all bats are scary animals hungry for blood. This misunderstanding means that many people are not interested in protecting bats. Many bats are even killed because people are fearful of them.

MYTH: BATS ARE SPOOKY

Along with ghosts and monsters, images of bats are often seen at Halloween. But bats are far from spooky. Vampire bats actually look after other bats in their colony by feeding them when they are sick. This caring behavior is rare in the natural world.

MYTH: BATS SUCK YOUR BLOOD

Only three species of bats eat blood to survive. These vampire bats are found in the Americas and approach animals during the night, when the animal is asleep and still. Unless you sleep outside, it's unlikely a vampire bat will come anywhere near you.

MYTH: BATS ARE RODENTS

Some people think of bats as flying mice. But bats are not even closely related to rodents. They belong to their own animal group, called Chiroptera, which means "hand-wing."

MYTH: BATS SPREAD DISEASES

Just like all other animals, bats can catch diseases. This is why it is important never to touch any wild animal, including bats. But the risk of catching a disease from a bat is no higher than the risk of catching something from a pet.

OTHER THREATS TO BATS

PESTICIDES

There are far fewer insects around now than before people started to use pesticides, which means there is less food for bats. The chemicals used on crops can also be poisonous to bats.

WHITE NOSES

In the Northeastern United States, large numbers of bats have been found with white fungus growing on their noses and wings. The fungus makes bats very sick and kills them. Some species, such as the little brown bat, are close to extinction.

COLLISIONS

Bats can also have accidents and fly into power lines, get hit by cars, and collide with wind turbines.

HUNTING

In some parts of the world bats are hunted for food. As the human population increases, there are more people hunting bats than ever before.

THERE ARE FEWER PLACES FOR BATS TO LIVE

Forests are home to many bats that roost and find food among the trees. But forests are disappearing quickly, since they are being cut down for wood and to make space for buildings and farms.

With fewer natural places to roost, many bats have adapted to live in buildings. Sometimes these buildings need work done, or they are demolished. This can disturb bats when they are roosting or hibernating.

LIVING WITH BATS

People and bats can live together without disturbing one another. If you find bats in the attic, the garage, or roof, it is important to remember:

A bat that is woken up during hibernation will use up a lot of its stored fat when finding a new home. It's unlikely it will survive the winter.

Bats reproduce slowly because they give birth to just one pup every year. This makes it hard for bats to recover when their numbers are in decline.

Bats won't damage your home by nibbling and chewing, and will not bring anything, such as prey, into the roost.

It is likely that bats will only be in your home for a few months, either to hibernate or to have babies.

Your home will never become infested because bats only give birth to one pup a year, so their numbers will not increase quickly.

Bats are protected by law, which means there are rules that say we can't harm them. If you find bats in your home, contact a bat conservation organization and they will be able to give you advice.

WHAT CAN YOU DO TO HELP?

SUPPORT A BAT CHARITY

You can become a member of a bat conservation organization and even adopt a bat to show your support.

FIND OUT MORE ABOUT BATS

You can learn more about the bats that live around you by going on a bat walk. Most organized walks use a bat detector to help you to hear bats and work out which species are nearby.

CHANGE THE WAY PEOPLE THINK ABOUT BATS

Bats are not scary. They are smart and social animals that like to go unnoticed. The more people understand bats, the more they will want to help them.

BECOME A SEED SPREADER

Just like a bat, you too can spread the seeds of important plants with a seed ball. Seed balls are little muddy balls that are full of seeds. Throw them into a green space and they will grow into plants that attract insects for bats to eat.

YOU WILL NEED:

Clay to protect the seeds from birds that might eat them.

Compost to give the seeds the nutrients they need to sprout.

Seeds such as borage, cornflower, night-scented stock, and evening primrose. Include as many of these as you like.

1.

In a large bowl or bucket, mix together four big handfuls of compost with a handful of clay and a handful of seeds.

2.

Little by little, add water until the mixture is soft enough so that you can squeeze it into balls.

3.

Roll the mixture in your hands to make marble-sized balls. Leave them in a sunny spot for at least three hours to dry.

4.

When your seed balls are dry, they can be thrown in your garden or planted in a pot. The best time to throw them is spring or fall.

You can also give seed balls as a gift. Wrap them up and make your own label with your favorite bat fact on it, so others will know why bats are great.

Nature will take care of the rest, so just wait and watch your bat-friendly plants grow!

GROW A BAT-FRIENDLY GARDEN

You can help bats by making your garden the perfect place for them to find food, water, and shelter. Growing a variety of plants will attract moths and flies for bats to eat. Follow these tips for a bat-friendly garden:

GIVE BATS SOME WATER

Bats like to live near water. Building a small pond will give bats a place to drink. Ponds also attract insects as many flies start their life in water as larvae.

GIVE BATS A HOME

You can buy or make your own bat house to give bats a safe place to roost. The houses need to be placed high up on tree trunks or on the side of a house.

AVOID USING CHEMICALS

Pesticides can be harmful to insects and bats. You can still have a beautiful garden without using chemicals.

KEEP PETS AWAY FROM BATS

Bats are frightened of cats. Keeping your cat indoors at night will keep bats safe and make bats more likely to visit your garden.

PLANT BAT-FRIENDLY PLANTS

These plants release their scent in the evening to attract moths, which bats love to eat during the night.

EVENING PRIMROSE

BUDDLEIA

HONEYSUCKLE

JASMINE

TOBACCO PLANT

NIGHT-SCENTED STOCK

BATS MAKE THE WORLD A BETTER PLACE

It's time to tell the world how fascinating these flying mammals really are. Understanding bats and doing what we can to protect them will ensure that we live in a world where plants are pollinated, seeds are spread, and ecosystems are healthy. Bats help lots of other animals and plants, but now bats need our help.

Let's share the real story about bats.

BAT INDEX

Penguin Random House

Author and Illustrator
Charlotte Milner

Editors Hélène Hilton, Becky Walsh
Consultant Dr. Rob Houston
US Senior Editor Shannon Beatty
Senior Producer Basia Ossowaska
Producers, Pre-Production Inderjit Bhullar, Sophie Chatellier
Jacket Coordinator Issy Walsh
Managing Editor Penny Smith
Managing Art Editor Mabel Chan
Creative Director Helen Senior
Publishing Director Sarah Larter

First American Edition, 2020
Published in the United States by DK Publishing
1450 Broadway, Suite 801, New York, NY 10018
Text and illustration copyright © Charlotte Milner, 2020
Design copyright © Dorling Kindersley Limited, 2020
DK, a Division of Penguin Random House LLC
20 21 22 23 24 10 9 8 7 6 5 4 3 2 1
001–316505–Feb/2020

DK books are available at special discounts when
purchased in bulk for sales promotions, premiums,
fund-raising, or educational use. For details, contact:
DK Publishing Special Markets, 1450 Broadway,
Suite 801, New York, NY 10018
SpecialSales@dk.com

Printed and bound in China

A WORLD OF IDEAS:
SEE ALL THERE IS TO KNOW

www.dk.com

ABOUT THE AUTHOR

Charlotte Milner creates books with playful designs to bring important information to young readers. Her books explore environmental conservation issues and inspire a love of the natural world.